Keeping it Cool

Written by
Melissa Boyd

Illustrated by
Vanessa Alexandre

Skills for Coping with Change

Some days I have worries
and sad feelings inside.

It can sometimes be hard to talk about and I may want to cry.

Finding positive ways to calm my emotions,
can relax how I feel.

Whether it's coloring, crafting, napping, or having a healthy meal.

It can help to write about my worries and
notice if there are any themes.

I can play a tune or make up a song, to describe what is bothering me.

I can play with bugs or plant a garden,
to enjoy time outside.

I can read a good book or play a fun game, like pretending that I'm a spy.

Painting, art, and drawing can also be lots of fun.

I can sit on my porch and think about my feelings, while basking in the sun.

Doing puzzles, board games, and chess with dad, always helps me to feel calm.

And I won't forget
about deep breathing,
which is an activity I
learned from my mom.

I can do something kind, like help with cooking, baking, and house chores.

I can also enjoy singing in the car, while going with mom to the store.

Spending time joking, laughing, and playing games, helps to keep my mood up.

It also feels good
playing with animals,
like my cute pup.

I can stay busy and be creative, as my worries float on by.

I can also enjoy playing with cool toys and making objects fly.

Thinking of fun times with family and friends, are good thoughts to focus on.

Remembering these times, helps me to feel cared for, important, loved, and warm.

It can also be relaxing to spend time making a gratitude list.

This can help me to have feelings of happiness, joy, and bliss.

When I'm ready to talk, I can find a trusting adult, like my mom and dad.

They are always ready to listen, whether I feel happy, upset, or sad.

I'm so glad I have many skills to help with keeping it cool.

With all my emotions, it's good to have helpful and fun coping tools.

Made in the USA
Monee, IL
11 July 2022

99460997R00019